W9-CBU-202

FOOTBALL LEGENDS

Troy Aikman

Terry Bradshaw

Jim Brown

Dan Marino

Joe Montana

Joe Namath

Walter Payton

Jerry Rice

Barry Sanders

Deion Sanders

Emmitt Smith

Steve Young

CHELSEA HOUSE PUBLISHERS

FOOTBALL LEGENDS

BARRY SANDERS

John F. Wukovits

Introduction by
Chuck Noll

CHELSEA HOUSE PUBLISHERS
New York · Philadelphia

Produced by Daniel Bial and Associates
New York, New York

Picture research by Alan Gottlieb
Cover illustration by Bill Vann

3 5 7 9 8 6 4 2

Wukovits, John, F.
    Barry Sanders / by John Wukovits
    p.   cm. — (Football legends)
    Includes bibliographical references and index.
    ISBN 0-7910-2459-8
    1. Sanders, Barry, 1968-   —Juvenile literature. 2. Football
    players—United States—Biography—Juvenile literature.
    3. Detroit Lions (Football team)—Juvenile literature.
    [1. Sanders, Barry, 1968-   . 2. Football players.
    3. Afro-Americans—Biography.] I. Title. II. Series.
    GV939.S18W85 1996
    796.332'092—dc20
    [B]   95-30121
                                                        CIP
                                                         AC

CONTENTS

A Winning Attitude

Chuck Noll

Don't ever fall into the trap of believing, "I could never do that. And I won't even try—I don't want to embarrass myself." After all, most top athletes had no idea what they could accomplish when they were young. A secret to the success of every star quarterback and sure-handed receiver is that they tried. If they had not tried, if they had not persevered, they would never have discovered how far they could go and how much they could achieve.

You can learn about trying hard and overcoming challenges by being a sports fan. Or you can take part in organized sports at any level, in any capacity. The student messenger at my high school is now president of a university. A reserve ballplayer who got very little playing time in high school now owns a very successful business. Both of them benefited from the lesson of perseverance that sports offers. The main point is that you don't have to be a Hall of Fame athlete to reap the benefits of participating in sports.

In math class, I learned that the whole is equal to the sum of its parts. But that is not always the case when you are dealing with people. Sports has taught me that the whole is either greater than or less than the sum of its parts, depending on how well the parts work together. And how the parts work together depends on how they really understand the concept of teamwork.

Most people believe that teamwork is a fifty-fifty proposition. But true teamwork is seldom, if ever, fifty-fifty. Teamwork is *whatever it takes to get the job done*. There is no time for the measurement of contributions, no time for anything but concentrating on your job.

One year, my Pittsburgh Steelers were playing the Houston Oilers in the Astrodome late in the season, with the division championship on the line. Our offensive line was hard hit by the flu, our starting quarterback was out with an injury, and we were having difficulty making a first down. There was tremendous pressure on our defense to perform well—and they rose to the occasion. If the players on the defensive unit had been measuring their contribution against the offense's contribution, they would have given up and gone home. Instead, with a "whatever it takes" attitude, they increased their level of concentration and performance, forced turnovers, and got the ball into field goal range for our offense. Thanks to our defense's winning attitude, we came away with a victory.

Believing in doing whatever it takes to get the job done is what separates a successful person from someone who is not as successful. Nobody can give you this winning outlook; you have to develop it. And I know from experience that it can be learned and developed on the playing field.

My favorite people on the football field have always been offensive linemen and defensive backs. I say this because it takes special people to perform well in jobs in which there is little public recognition when they are doing things right but are thrust into the spotlight as soon as they make a mistake. That is exactly what happens to a lineman whose man sacks the quarterback or a defensive back who lets his receiver catch a touchdown pass. They know the importance of being part of a group that believes in teamwork and does not point fingers at one another.

Sports can be a learning situation as much as it can be fun. And that's why I say, "Get involved. Participate."

CHUCK NOLL, the Pittsburgh Steelers head coach from 1969–91, led his team to four Super Bowl victories—the most by any coach. Widely respected as an innovator on both offense and defense, Noll was inducted into the Pro Football Hall of Fame in 1993.

1

"LET'S WIN AND GO HOME"

Christmas Eve, 1989, brought few good tidings on the gridiron for members of the Detroit Lions. Heading into this final game of the regular season, a road contest against the inept Atlanta Falcons, the woeful team had stumbled to a dismal 6-9 record. Not only would the playoffs once again begin without them but they seemed a distant hope for 1990 as well. The players trotted onto the field, barely able to hear cheers or taunts from the less than 8,000 diehard fans sprinkling the huge stadium, determined to win more from a sense of pride than anything else.

One other factor impelled them to give their best effort. The team's remarkable rookie running back, Barry Sanders, had scampered through and around enemy defenses to accu-

Barry Sanders charges around would-be tackler Robert Brown in a 1989 game against the Green Bay Packers. Sanders gained 184 yards on 30 carries in the game.

mulate over 1,300 yards. His breathtaking runs, created by an enviable combination of quickness and tremendous leg strength, produced mounds of praise from opponents left in his wake.

"You have to tackle him with good technique," explained All-Pro linebacker for the Chicago Bears, Mike Singletary. "If you try to blast him, chances are he'll spin out of it and you'll end up looking a little silly."

If Sanders could add another 169 yards in this game he would overtake the current rushing leader, Christian Okoye of the Kansas City Chiefs, and snare an NFL rushing title in his first season, an amazing feat for a newcomer to the crushing world of professional football. Since Okoye had already completed his final game, Sanders controlled his own fate.

He started quickly, using his spectacular ability to slip out of tacklers' grasps to pile up yardage. Sweeping around end or bursting through the line with lightning speed, Sanders steadily narrowed the gap between himself and Okoye. With would-be Atlanta defenders clutching nothing but air near the dodging, twisting Sanders, the rookie crashed into the end zone in the second quarter for a 25-yard touchdown run, added a 17-yard score in the third quarter, and capped another in a season-long string of unforgettable performances by crossing the goal line with an 18-yard scamper early in the fourth quarter to put the Lions up, 31–10. Confident that victory was secure, Sanders settled on the bench to watch the remaining ten minutes.

Suddenly, momentum reverted to the Falcons, who rammed across two quick touchdowns against a confused Lions defense. Though only one minute remained, the Lions

lead had dwindled to a single score, 31–24, but if they could simply avoid fumbling and run out the clock, victory would be assured.

Just then an assistant informed Lions head coach, Wayne Fontes, that Sanders's total yards stood at 158—11 shy of surpassing Okoye. Fontes walked over to his prize rookie.

In the last game of the 1989 season, Barry Sanders takes a handoff from quarterback Bob Gagliano and finds the hole for a 17-yard touchdown.

"You're 10 yards from catching Okoye. Do you want to go back in?" Fontes asked Sanders.

The rookie's response stunned Fontes. "Coach, let's just win it and go home." When Fontes wondered if Sanders's contract contained a bonus clause for winning the rushing title, Sanders quietly added, "Coach, give the ball to Tony [Paige]. Let's just win it and go home."

This was not the first time Sanders had remained on the bench rather than add to his personal totals, and in a league filled with glory-hounds and headline seekers, the rookie from Kansas represented a refreshing change. Winning was all that mattered to him—not yardage or touchdowns.

"The things that are fun to me," he explained after the game, "are and always will be the competition, and going out and trying to win. If you do that, then big plays and statistics will take care of themselves." He added that "When everyone is out for statistics—you know, individual fulfillment—that's when trouble starts. I don't want to ever fall victim to that."

When a sports reporter asked him if he was not even a little bit irritated by losing the rushing title by a mere 11 yards, Sanders replied, "I satisfied my ego last season [when he captured college football's most prestigious award, the Heisman Trophy]."

Though Barry Sanders had played an entire season, football observers around the league had only seen the talented runner who transformed the field between the goal lines into a magical stage upon which he performed his wizardry. With these unassuming statements, though, the world of professional football received a glimpse inside Barry Sanders, a quiet, thoughtful man to whom family, religion, hard work, and the desire to excel for his teammates meant more than individual glory. Had onlookers gazed a little closer, they would have noticed these characteristics first appeared in Wichita, Kansas, Barry Sanders's birthplace.

2

A Lot Inside

Barry Sanders was born on July 16, 1968, the seventh of eleven children born to William and Shirley Sanders, strong-willed parents who were determined their offspring grow up with a firm set of values. William Sanders, who toiled in the hot, grimy world of the roofer, emphasized hard work, discipline, and hatred of waste—all necessary ingredients when eight girls, three boys, and two parents live together in a small three-bedroom home in Wichita, Kansas.

Two rules existed in the Sanders household. "Rule No. 1: Never disobey Dad. Rule No. 2: Never forget Rule No. 1."

If Dad needed help roofing, Barry and his two older brothers, Boyd and Byron, knew what kind of day lay ahead for them—sweating in the blazing sun while they handled hot tar. The only thing that could make an already miserable day worse was for them to complain, an action sure to bring the wrath of their father.

Barry with his Pee Wee football team. He's number 35, in the front row center.

The boys also knew if they asked for money for helping, or wondered why they did not earn an allowance when their friends did, their father would sharply respond, "Your allowance is that I pay the bills around here." Barry could not get over the fact that many of his schoolmates received an allowance "just for being alive."

"We were raised to use what you have and not go around looking for more," explained Sanders. "We were taught not to be greedy or obsessed with what you couldn't have. It's a trait that comes from not having very much outside and a lot inside."

While absorbing a work ethic from his father, Sanders learned how to treat people from his mother, a devoutly religious person who, according to Sanders, "doesn't talk to hear herself talk. She would rather see other people happy than herself. I've never heard her curse. I've never seen her take a drink. She is a Christian woman. A real one." Quiet by nature and thus more like his mother than his father, Sanders has tried to follow her example all his life, but admits he has a tough act to follow. When asked if he falls short of her standards, he replies, "Most people do."

Sanders entered sports for the first time in fourth grade. After receiving an electric football set for Christmas from one of his sisters, Sanders played with the game for hours, completely fascinated by the tiny figures that bounced and vibrated across the metal field. "I identified with the running back," he mentioned, and before long Sanders transferred his interest from the metal playing field to an outdoor one.

Though he had never donned a helmet, Sanders signed up to play football with the

Beech Red Barons, a team in the Greater Wichita Youth Football League. Almost from the beginning he heard the taunts that he was too small to play the game. Even his father, at first, thought his brother Byron held the true family talent.

On the day of Barry's first game, his father instead walked to the field where Byron's team was playing. While he watched, a friend ran over and yelled, "Hey, Bill. You ought to see what Barry's doing down on the other field!" When Mr. Sanders wondered what he meant, the friend explained, "He scored three touchdowns already. He's running past everybody."

The stunned father muttered, "Barry? Barry can't even play football."

Mr. Sanders quickly learned he was wrong. Barry began to refine his talent in wild pickup games that sometimes featured as many as twenty players on the field for each side. Whoever ran with the ball either had to be quick, or find himself at the bottom of a huge pile of tacklers.

"Because I was smaller I had to learn real fast to avoid getting hit," stated Sanders. As his elementary school years unwound and he played in more of these contests, Sanders started piecing together the electrifying style that eventually lifted him to the professional leagues.

Many teenagers, especially during their junior high school years, begin questioning adult-imposed rules and attempt to assert their individuality. Sanders was no different. He once told a Detroit sports writer that he was "always doing something wrong. I was loudmouthed. Fighting. Discipline problem."

In ninth grade he called his gym teacher a

Barry was also a fine basketball player for his Wichita North High School team.

punk in front of the entire class because the teacher did not select him for the school's basketball team, an action that earned him a quick suspension. "I can't believe I did that," he now says.

Compared to other youths his age, Sanders was far from being a major problem, but coming from the religious atmosphere established by his mother, he probably believed he was a bit wild. Guidance from his mother and older brother Boyd, and a love of sports, helped push this rather tame rebelliousness out of Sanders.

Sanders jumped wholeheartedly into sports at Wichita North High School. While most friends partied or drank with the boys on weekends, Sanders and his brother Byron ran up and down the steps of a nearby football stadium. Though basketball was his first love—he lettered three years in the sport—Sanders applied himself equally as hard to football.

He had to, for the doubters circled around him like vultures because of his small size. Standing approximately 5'7" and weighing less than 150 pounds, many thought he could never make an impact in a game featuring monstrous lineman and tacklers who loved to crush a runner's bones. One person, though, knew he could shine.

"I never knew how good I could be then because everyone was always telling me I was too small," explained Sanders. "Everyone but my father. He told me I could be great. I know people think that was just a father talking, but he always told me the truth."

The high school's defensive backfield coach, Dennis Brunner, recalled a time Barry's father walked up to him during a scrimmage in his son's sophomore year and bluntly told him Barry "was going to be a football player. I was pleased with Byron, but the father must have sensed something special in Barry."

As would often be the case in Sanders's career, he placed humility and loyalty ahead of statistics and glory. When head coach Bob Shepler wanted to insert Barry at tailback, Barry objected since his brother Byron held the starting job at that position. Rather than showcasing his own talent at the running slot, Sanders started at defensive back and wingback for the team.

In Barry's senior year, Dale Burkholder took over as head coach. He not only thought that Sanders was too small to be effective as a running back, but preferred a halfback who ran straight at the line instead of in the zigzag style favored by Sanders. From the stands, William Sanders's booming voice would bellow to the coaches, "Play him! Let him run!" But his son remained on the bench whenever the offense took the field.

Finally, with only six games remaining on the 1985 schedule, Burkholder inserted Sanders at tailback. The diminutive runner carved up the field like it was his personal playground. Swerving from side to side, darting underneath tacklers' lunges, the senior accumulated 274 yards and 4 touchdowns in leading his team to victory. By season's end Sanders totaled over 1,400 yards—an average of more than 230 yards per game—earning him spots on the first team All-City and All-State teams.

Coach Brunner watched, practically speechless at the magic wrought by Sanders. "I can still see him out there doing things that seem impossible. As fast as he was, he could stop on a dime and reverse his field before the defense could react. He made some dazzling runs and was fabulous all year."

In the final game against Emporia High, Sanders tore through the defense for over 300 yards in helping his team build a huge lead. Burkholder noticed in the fourth quarter that Sanders only needed thirty yards to become the league's top rusher, but Sanders declined the chance to return.

Though he could create a surge of emotion that swept through the stands with his running talent, off the field the shy Sanders preferred anonymity, especially when it came to girls. He felt out of place at parties and became tongue-tied around females. In his senior year, he tried to remove his name from the list of homecoming nominees, but to no avail. The introspective star won.

Longtime friend Mark McCormick recalled the night of the dance. "There's a picture I have of him [Sanders] and the homecoming queen that night. You should see it. She looks so happy, all smiles—and Barry looks like he's constipated."

Burkholder and his staff had to work hard to attract the notice of college recruiters for Sanders, since he had started so few games. They sent a highlight film to area universities, but this failed to stir much interest. Big-time coaches had already scouted other runners, and they were not much interested in a small tailback who had only played in six games.

"His size was the big thing," said Brunner. "He wasn't tall, and a lot of the recruiters didn't feel he could hold much more weight on his compact body."

The University of Nebraska returned the highlight film without even viewing it. The University of Oklahoma mailed one letter to Sanders, but never followed up on it. Other universities declined to send information.

Sanders refused to become disheartened and believed he simply needed the chance to prove his detractors wrong. "It's amazing to me how much attention coaches and scouts pay to size," he later explained. "I think that's where a lot of them fail. The fact that most of the big schools ignored me gave me incentive to show them that it's not all about size."

Finally, an offer rolled in. After studying Sander's highlight film, Oklahoma State University assistant coach George Walstad convinced head coach Pat Jones to give the Wichita tailback a scholarship as a kick returner and backup for their sensational runner, Thurman Thomas. Sanders, his short but heady high school football career over, moved on to the next level of excellence.

3

"THE CREAM RISES TO THE TOP"

Barry Sanders started his college career in August 1986, when he traveled to Stillwater, Oklahoma, for summer practice. Prospects for playing did not appear great. Not only was he an untested freshman with a short, although spectacular, high school football record, but on the depth charts he stood behind All-American junior tailback, Thurman Thomas, who had gained an eye-popping total of 1,650 yards the year before.

His lowly status did not bother Sanders. "I was completely content with what I was doing there. I wasn't expected to play. But I remember my father always saying that the cream rises to the top."

As he did in both the Wichita Youth Football League and in high school, Sanders quickly impressed people who really were not anticipating much from him. His wizardry in shaking off

Barry Sanders was attracted to Oklahoma State University because of the fine reputation of its business school.

tacklers, whether as a backup runner for Thomas or as the team's kickoff and punt return man, forced Cowboy head coach Pat Jones to insert him into the game more frequently.

"The more he got involved in things, the more he jumped out at us," declared Jones. "We had already decided to use him that [freshman] year as a kick returner, to take the heat off Thurman. But we began realizing that we had to concoct some things to get him the ball."

Sanders ended his freshman season with impressive statistics, considering Thurman Thomas received most of the playing time. He compiled a 23.7 yard average in 7 kickoff returns, added another 43 yards running back punts, and rushed for 325 yards and 2 touchdowns in 74 carries. Though the nation's sports writers still focused the spotlight on Thomas and National Football League scouts came to Stillwater to chart the gifted junior, Sanders steadily and quietly drew the attention of his coaches.

He worked hard in the off season to add bulk to his small frame. Repeated visits to the weight room, where Sanders concentrated mainly on squat-lifts and bench-presses, added another twenty pounds of muscle, particularly in his thighs and legs, which now resembled sturdy tree trunks. Sanders entered the 1987 season a muscular 200 pounds, and felt confident he would contribute even more to the Cowboy offense.

His feats lived up to his expectations. Though once again playing in Thomas's shadow, Sanders almost doubled his yards rushing to 622 while tallying 9 touchdowns, although he only carried the ball 37 times more than the year before. Three times he rushed for over 100 yards in a game, and he expanded his offensive arsenal by catching 4 passes for 58 yards and 1 score.

More importantly, Sanders led the National Collegiate Athletic Association (NCAA) in kickoff returns with a heady 31.3 return average, captured second in the nation with a 15.2 punt return average, and scored 4 touchdowns while returning the ball.

Thomas turned in another All-American season. At one point he had been projected as a high first-round draft pick, but a knee injury his junior year dropped him to a mid-second round choice of the Buffalo Bills. Thomas quickly established himself as a pro star and helped the Bills go to four straight Super Bowls. Meantime, praise started pouring in for the talented sophomore, who was named to the *Sporting News* All-American team as kick returner. Observers eagerly looked ahead to Sanders's junior year, when he would take over the first string tailback slot.

Only one disturbing aspect menaced a bright future—rumors swirled about campus that some players had received money, fancy cars, and plush jobs to play at Oklahoma State. If true, the NCAA might impose sanctions on the team. Though Barry drove an eight-year-old car and in the summer bagged groceries at a supermarket a cloud of doubt hovered over the team.

Barry applied himself off the field as well. One reason Oklahoma State appealed to him was the reputation of its business school, and now that he had been admitted he refused to duck classes other football players might have

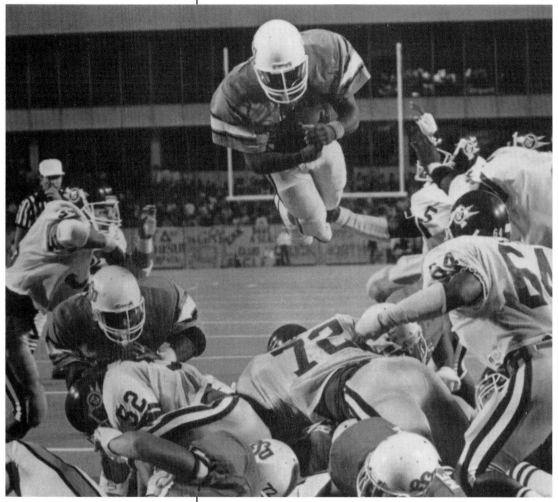

Thurman Thomas was Oklahoma State's starting tailback in 1986 and 1987. He would later go on to star with the Buffalo Bills.

avoided because of their strict requirements. His mother's emphasis on education had Barry looking to his future, whether or not it included football.

In spite of establishing himself as a player to watch, Sanders remained the same low-key, soft-spoken individual that he had been in high school. His teammates knew they could count on Barry swinging credit their way instead of hogging all the glory, and they respected him for the decent manner in which he conducted himself. When one close friend experienced financial problems in school, Sanders immediately gave him half of the money he was getting from his own football scholarship.

"If I had a kid," gushed the team's quarterback, Mike Gundy, "I'd want him to grow up to be like Barry. Not because of his great athletic ability, but because of the kind of person he is."

4

"IT'S NO SHOW— IT'S BARRY"

Sanders did not automatically move into the starting tailback slot once Thurman was gone. Coach Jones stated that because of his inexperience as a full-time player, Sanders would have to earn that position.

He worked hard during summer practice. The teams already featured an explosive offensive unit, relying on the accurate passing of quarterback Mike Gundy to receiver Hart Lee Dykes. Since most of the offensive linemen who had cleared holes for Thurman Thomas were back, Barry's electric style could nicely complement the aerial attack and keep opposing defenses guessing as to which weapon would be coming at them. Before the season opened, Sanders had captured the first-string slot.

By the season's third game, Coach Jones knew that he possessed one of the most productive offensive threats in the nation. In the

Once Barry Sanders was named to a starter's role on the Cowboys, he showed he was the best running back in college.

Cowboys' first two games, a 52–20 victory over the University of Miami, Ohio, and 52–15 trouncing of top-ten rated Texas A&M, Sanders picked up 335 yards and 4 touchdowns, including a 100-yard kickoff return against the Aggies. Sanders accelerated in the third game, a 56–35 pasting of the University of Tulsa, by scoring 5 times and setting a new school record with 304 rushing yards.

Fans poured into Lewis Field in Stillwater to watch the new phenom, who was soon playing before more than 50,000 crazed supporters. Members of the national press, accustomed to finding their way to Oklahoma State to record Thurman Thomas's exploits, now filtered back to take a look at his successor. They were as impressed as Coach Jones.

"He's the most explosive guy I've ever seen," declared Jones. "He sees an opening, and he can be at full-speed, bam, just like that. Plus he's so strong and tough that people just can't tackle him."

Sanders garnered more national headlines over the next four games. The Cowboys warmed up for a showdown against unbeaten and perennial college powerhouse University of Nebraska, by defeating the University of Colorado, 41–21, behind Barry's 174 yards and 4 touchdowns. Though Sanders duplicated his 4 scores the following Saturday, the Cowboy defense was more than outmatched by Nebraska's huge linemen and swift runners, who propelled the Cornhuskers to a 63–42 win over Sanders and Oklahoma State. Though a defeat, sportswriters conspicuously pointed out that the 189 rushing yards gained by Sanders pushed him past the 1,000-yard mark—and six games still remained on the schedule!

The Cowboys rebounded with two successive victories, 49–21 against University of Missouri and 45–27 against Kansas State University. While Sanders was "held" to only 154 yards in the first contest, he tore though the Kansas State defense for 320 yards and 3 touchdowns, establishing a new NCAA record with his second 300-yard effort. Talk surfaced of a Heisman Trophy for Sanders—the award given to college football's most valuable player—even though only eight juniors had ever captured the prestigious statue. Four games remained on the Cowboy schedule. Should Sanders continue his incredible pace, the award ceremony could become a formality.

At 7-1, the Cowboys retained hopes of winning a Big Eight Conference championship and finishing among the top ten teams in the nation, goals that meant more to Sanders than the Heisman Trophy. Fortunately, by helping his team Sanders also locked up the Heisman. In front of 50,000 crazed home fans, he added 215 yards in a heartbreaking, final-minute loss to cross-state rival University of Oklahoma, 31–28. The Cowboys took out their revenge the next week by thrashing Kansas, 63–24, with Sanders again dominating headlines by registering his third 300-yard game of the season as well as scoring 5 touchdowns.

Soon after winning the Heisman Trophy in 1988, Barry posed with his mother, father, and five sisters.

The Heisman Trophy is awarded to the top collegiate football player each year. Barry was in Japan when it was announced that he had won the coveted award.

The attention of the sports world had turned toward Stillwater and its explosive back, particularly when Sanders raced to 293 yards and 4 touchdowns the next week in a win against Iowa State University. Some sportswriters declared the Heisman race all but over and that Barry's chief rivals, quarterbacks Troy Aikman from UCLA and Rodney Peete of USC, stood little chance of overtaking the Oklahoma State tailback.

Normally, nominees for the Heisman head to New York the weekend that the winner is announced, but along with his teammates Sanders boarded a plane to play Texas Tech in the Coca-Cola Classic in Tokyo, Japan. Sports reporters from the United States shadowed his every move in the Japanese capital, but Sanders tried his best to ignore the notoriety and adulation.

"It's just not that big a deal for me," he told a writer from *Sports Illustrated.* "And it's not really fair to so many other people. People take sports way too seriously. To some of them sports is a god, which is wrong."

Instead, Barry worried that he project the right image to young people. He understood that large numbers of American teens grow up without role models, and he knew he had "an opportunity to be a positive influence on young people. I have never used drugs. I try to study and stay out of trouble."

Even in festive Tokyo. One time a group of players spotted Sanders as they were leaving the hotel to sample Tokyo's nightclubs. When they asked if he wanted to go along, Barry refused, saying, "No, I want to stay in and study."

One day before the Heisman winner was to be made public, Oklahoma State publicist Steve Buzzard asked Sanders if he would appear the next day on a satellite hookup from the CBS Television studio in Tokyo to the Downtown Athletic Club in New York City, where his parents and other family members would be assembled. Sanders, who was tiring of all the demands being made on his time, replied that he would rather avoid it since it was game day.

At the urging of teammates, Sanders agreed to do the hookup. As Coach Jones explained, it was not that Barry downplayed the honor of receiving the Heisman, but "he'd prefer not to go through the things associated with it."

As the link was established between Barry in Tokyo and his parents and brother Byron in New York shortly before the announcement, excitement swept the faces of his proud parents and brother. Barry, on the other hand, calmly sat in a chair and awaited the results. They were overwhelmingly in his favor, with Sanders receiving close to eighty percent of all first-place votes cast and far outdistancing Rodney Peete and Troy Aikman. He became only the ninth junior to receive college football's highest honor.

Sanders politely accepted the award and told a television audience that he only deserved part of the acclaim. "My teammates worked so hard. It's just hard to see myself getting a lot of credit and seeing those guys get pushed aside."

Packed together in another room, Oklahoma State's offensive linemen cried tears of joy over Barry's award and his words honoring them. While the lumbering football players celebrated with loud yells and hearty backslapping, guard Jason Kidder referred to Barry's calm demeanor at a time of high excitement. "It's for real, it's no show. It's Barry." What was also Barry was the show he put on for 54,000 curious Japanese spectators who piled into the Tokyo Dome for their first glimpse of American college football later that day. In a seesaw affair, Oklahoma State topped Texas Tech, 45–42, behind Barry's finest collegiate showing. The newest Heisman winner ran for a career-high 332 yards and 4 touchdowns on 44 carries.

Only one game remained in Barry's career. Recognizing the Cowboy's fine 9-2 record, organizers of the Holiday Bowl in San Diego, California, invited Sanders and the Oklahoma State team to take on 11-1 University of Wyoming on December 30, 1988. Sanders again ran wild and led his team to a decisive 62–14 victory. When he left the game at the end of the third quarter, Barry had tallied 5 touchdowns en route to amassing 222 yards, only 4 short of the bowl record. Coach Jones asked Sanders if he wanted to re-enter the game to pick up the needed amount, but as usual Sanders declined so that other players could see action. "The record was not important to me," he explained to sportswriters. "The important thing was that we won."

The Holiday Bowl capped an extraordinary season for Sanders, during which he set or tied twenty-four NCAA records. His 2,628 rushing yards shattered Marcus Allen's seven-year-old

NCAA single-season record by almost 300 yards—and Sanders rushed 59 fewer times than Allen! He set new marks for average yards rushing per game (238.9), most rushing touchdowns in a season (37), and smashed Byron R. "Whizzer" White's 51-year-old record of most all-purpose yards in a season (3,250).

Barry's incredible output in 1988—a season that began with Coach Jones declaring that Sanders had to prove himself a worthy successor to Thurman Thomas—doubled Thomas's totals from the year before. Jones admitted his junior Heisman Trophy winner compiled a season unlike any he had ever seen. "It's like a baseball player hitting 75 homeruns, stealing 150 bases, winning 25 games, and driving in 200 runs, all in the same year."

5

"WHEN YOU GET TO HIM, HE'S NOT THERE"

The main issue to be settled after Barry's remarkable 1988 season was whether to turn professional or to remain in school. His mother and sisters urged him to stay at Oklahoma State for his senior year to complete his education, but his father and brothers argued with equal vigor that Barry should dash to the pros. His father doubted that Barry could improve much on his Heisman year, and should Sanders play another season for Coach Jones, he faced the risk of an injury that might keep him out of the professional ranks. Besides, with a large family placing heavy financial burdens on Barry's parents, the prospect of his earning a large salary proved hard to resist.

When the persistent rumors that the NCAA was going to censor Oklahoma State's football program appeared to be accurate, Barry decided

Coach Wayne Fontes shows off the jersey of the number one pick in the 1989 draft. The Detroit Lions gave Sanders the number 20 out of respect to their former star Billy Sims who had just retired due to injuries.

to ask NFL Commissioner Pete Rozelle for permission to enter the draft. Rozelle approved the request, sending NFL scouts and coaches hastening to get a better look at the phenom.

Among the coaches at an NFL workout for possible draftees was Detroit Lions head coach, Wayne Fontes. He knew Sanders possessed a multitude of talent, but wondered if the relatively small back was quick enough for what the Lions needed. Sanders dispelled that fear by burning up the forty-yard dash in 4.39 seconds. An impressed Fontes wondered why he had doubted that aspect of Sanders, since "in all the film we saw, we never saw anyone catch him. That should have told us something."

Any question marks in Fontes's mind evaporated when Sanders leaped a startling forty inches in the vertical leap. Kansas City head coach Marty Schottenheimer had only seen one other player jump that distance, so he asked Sanders to try one more time. Fontes later explained that Sanders "just went up and up. When he finally touched down, ever so gently, I looked up and saw how high he'd jumped [41½ inches]." Labeling the feat "Michael Jordan stuff," Fontes turned to his assistant coaches and mentioned, "Gentlemen, it's over. We can all go home. He's coming to Detroit."

The Dallas Cowboys opened the NFL draft by choosing UCLA quarterback Troy Aikman. When the Green Bay Packers opted for Michigan State lineman Tony Mandarich, a relieved Fontes selected Sanders, making him the third player taken overall. In the midst of yet another rebuilding year following a lengthy string of miserable seasons, the Lions later added Barry's Heisman rival, quarterback Rodney Peete of the

University of Southern California.

Contract difficulties delayed Barry's arrival with the team. The Lions offered a substantial amount, but lawyers hired by Sanders's father argued the contract stood nowhere near the level that a Heisman winner should receive. Bitter accusations flowed back and forth, causing Sanders to miss training camp and every exhibition game. Finally, three days before the start of the regular season, Barry and the Lions hammered out a lucrative five-year, 5.9 millions dollar contract, with an additional signing bonus of 2.1 millions dollars. Sanders promptly donated ten percent of his signing bonus—

Detroit was not a good team in 1989, losing eight of their first nine games. Sanders was its prime offensive threat, and when teams ganged up on him—as the New York Giants did here— the Lions had little else to try.

$210,000—to the Paradise Baptist Church in Wichita, then headed to Detroit for the start of his professional career.

Sanders had to wonder what kind of reception he would receive from victory-starved Lions supporters. The local media and many fans had already criticized him for holding out through the entire exhibition season before he had even donned a Lions uniform. Was he motivated by money? critics asked.

One game erased any unpleasant thoughts. On September 10, over 60,000 excited fans flocked to the Pontiac Silverdome for the season opener against the Phoenix Cardinals, eager to get a look at the high-priced rookie and anxious to get results from a runner who had never played a down in the professional ranks.

Sanders made his entrance into the NFL with 5:36 left in the third quarter and the team trailing. Fontes walked over to Sanders, who had been quietly watching from the sidelines, and said, "Relax. Be the kind of back we know you can be."

As Sanders trotted onto the field, the Silverdome crowd rose to its feet in a thundering ovation that seemed to shake the walls of the stadium. "I was in the huddle and suddenly I heard this roar," explained Lions quarterback Bob Gagliano. "I didn't know what they were cheering about. And then I saw him coming."

The noise was so deafening that Gagliano had to call timeout to avoid a Lions' penalty for delay of game. On the first snap, Sanders acted as a decoy. On the next play Gagliano handed off to Sanders, who smashed through the Cardinals for his first eighteen NFL yards. Gagliano called Sanders's number for the rest of

the drive, which Sanders capped with a three-
yard plunge into the end zone for his first professional touchdown.

One Detroit sportswriter, Mitch Albom, wrote
that, "The effect was undeniable. It was
Christmas morning. New Year's Eve. Whenever
he touched the ball it was as if 100,000 volts
spit through the Silverdome seats. . . . Here was
a desert thirst being splashed by water."

Though Sanders only had time to learn one
play, the off-tackle run, he still left Cardinal
tacklers in his wake in compiling 71 yards for
the game. Despite suffering a 16–13 loss from a
late Phoenix field goal, Fontes raved afterward
that Sanders "ran the same play over and over
and over again, and they all looked different.
That's the sign of a great back."

In postgame interviews, Sanders explained
that he was not nervous in his first appearance
and felt NFL tacklers hit about the same as good
college defenders. When asked if he was pleased
with his performance, Sanders replied, "We lost.
So I guess it wasn't good enough."

Sanders was off and running. After adding
57 yards in 12 carries against the New York
Giants, Sanders tore through the Chicago Bears
for 126 yards, though he suffered a bruised hip
when he decided to forego wearing hip pads.
The next week, he gained only one yard in five
carries before being removed because of the
injury. "I definitely learned why the Lord invent-
ed hip pads," said a chastened Sanders, who
vowed never to let that happen again.

Midway through his rookie year, when he
totaled 184 yards in an overtime loss to Green
Bay, Sanders had made his mark on the league.
Professionals used similar words of praise that

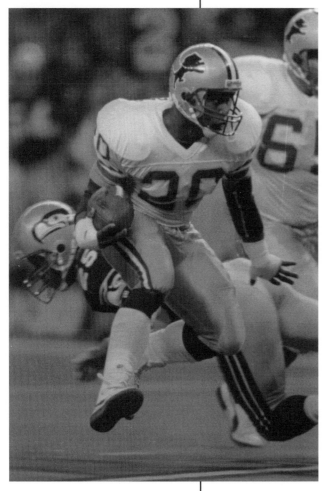

In the last game of the 1990 season, Sanders gained only 23 yards on nine carries against the Seattle Seahawks. But that was enough to make him the season's top NFL rusher.

college opponents had spoken. Green Bay linebacker Brian Noble, after trying unsuccessfully to hem in Sanders, exclaimed, "Usually, when you get to him, he's not there anymore." Chicago Bears defensive end Trace Armstrong remarked, "I remember bracing myself to hit him. I knew I had him. But he just stopped and turned, and he was gone. He's like a little sports car. He can stop on a dime and go zero to 60 in seconds." The Minnesota Vikings had such a hard time bringing Sanders down that they accused him of spraying his jersey with silicone to make it slippery. Officials, however, found nothing when they inspected Barry's uniform during a timeout.

While the Lions stumbled to an atrocious 1-8 record, Sanders continued his hectic pace. By the traditional Thanksgiving Day game at the Silverdome, Barry became the first NFL runner to hit 1,000 yards for the season.

Only the poor won-loss record marred Barry's fine rookie year. He would gladly have traded in chunks of yards for a few victories. The offense began jelling, however, in the Lions' final seven games, with Barry leading the way to six victories, including 145 yards rushing against the Cleveland Browns, 120 yards rushing and two touchdowns against the Bears, and his final tally of 158 yards against Atlanta.

At last, hope had arrived for Detroit fans. Here was the runner who would be a factor for years to come and who could sweep the Lions into the playoffs. "Restore the Roar!" they yelled, and pointed with glee to their prize rookie who had only missed out on the NFL rushing title because he had chosen to sit out the closing minutes against Atlanta. Sanders and his teammates looked forward to 1990.

Barry's unique talents earned him the Associated Press 1989 Offensive Rookie of the Year award, landed him in the Pro Bowl, and made him the sole rookie to make the *Sporting News* All-Pro team. To show his appreciation, Sanders gave each Lions offensive lineman a $10,000 Rolex wristwatch.

His season was all the more extraordinary when you consider that he missed training camp, ran behind a weak offensive line, and worked out of the Lions run-and-shoot offense, one more suited to passing than running. Even with such restrictions, Barry's agility bubbled to the surface and confounded opposing defenses.

Chicago Bear Hall of Fame running back, Walter Payton, bluntly declared, "I don't know if I was ever that good." Lions defensive coordinator, Woody Widenhofer, explained that Barry's huge legs enabled him to burst through the line and into the secondary, where his speed turned him into a menace. "He's a freight train going through the line, then a bug-in-a-rug when he gets in the secondary," added Widenhofer.

Sanders simply explained his year by saying he improvised as he went along and, like sandlot days, relied on natural talent and explosiveness. "When I run with the football, it's this feeling, man, I can't really describe it. It's like being a kid and playing tag, and that fear you have. I'm just trying to avoid the guy out there tagging me, that's all."

The Lions opened the 1990 season brimming with confidence. It was short-lived. In the opener against the Tampa Bay Bucs, the team committed basic errors and sputtered on both offense and defense, dropping a 38–21 game to one of the weakest teams in the NFL. The rest of the season showed little improvement as opposing defenses assigned two or more men to watch Sanders. Though the Lions' record dropped to 6-10, the elusive Sanders still rushed for 1,304 yards and captured the NFL's rushing title, the first Detroit Lions running back to accomplish that feat since Byron "Whizzer" White fifty years earlier.

What amazed onlookers was that many of Barry's most exciting runs gained few, if any, yards. Former Lions offensive coordinator Mouse Davis watched Sanders chew up numerous defenses, but the run he most remembers "was when he took the handoff and the Bears were all over him. He spun, went down into a kind of one-legged squat, spun again, made a guy miss him and ran for just a two-yard loss. Absolutely spectacular."

Though earning adulation for his on-field heroics, Barry zealously tried to maintain a semblance of normalcy off the field. While driving with his close friend, Lions safety William White, Sanders was pulled over to the side by a police officer for speeding. When the officer looked at Barry's driver's license, he wondered if he was "the Barry Sanders?"

Instead of cheerfully answering yes, Sanders quietly replied, "Um, my name is Barry

Sanders." The officer handed him the ticket, thinking the driver was someone with the same name.

"You big dummy!" White exclaimed. "All you had to do is tell him who you were and you would have gotten off!"

"Nah, I can't do that," said Sanders as they drove away. He has always felt uncomfortable being considered different or better than others simply because of his football talent. "It doesn't make any sense," he claims. "I'm an average person, I really am." He asserts that when athletes start believing they are "special" because of their skill, that is where problems begin. "People treat them differently and you start thinking you're better than everybody else. You're not."

He politely gives autographs, especially to kids, but wonders why his name on a piece of paper makes the paper any more valuable. He will sometimes ask that question of adults who request autographs, and "most of the time they can't answer. That's amazing to me, man."

When a local Jeep dealership offered Sanders a new Jeep to come in and sign autographs for 1½ hours, he declined. Sanders avoids the spotlight whenever he can, and since he already owned a car, he did not need another one

"People think Barry is putting on an act with that humble stuff," mentions White. "But I'm telling you, he really is that humble."

6

THE MEASURING STICK

The Lions rewarded Sanders by giving him a new contract before the 1991 season began. Sanders asked that a clause be included that handed a $10,000 bonus to the offensive linemen in any year in which Sanders rushed for 1,000 yards. With Barry's track record, that extra money seemed almost guaranteed for his blockers.

Fontes also was determined to use Sanders more frequently in 1991. The subject of heavy criticism from reporters and fans for handing the ball to Sanders—the most exciting runner in football—an average of less than fifteen times each game in 1990, Fontes modified the shoot-and-run to include more draw plays and other schemes designed to get the pigskin to Barry. After ten games, Sanders led the NFC in rushing with 902 yards and the reinvigorated 6-4 Lions were finally contending for a playoff spot.

Barry Sanders stretches during minicamp after the 1990 season. Before the 1991 season started, Detroit signed him to a new contract.

A game in early October against the Minnesota Vikings typified the new spirit that coursed through the Lions team. With only seven minutes remaining in the contest, the Lions trailed 20–3 after playing a sloppy three quarters. Past Lions teams, as any long-suffering Detroit fan could have explained, would have gone through the motions until game's end. Expecting more of the same, many of the angry spectators headed toward the Silverdome exits. Rodney Peete startled everyone, though, with a 68-yard touchdown pass to Robert Clark to narrow the gap, 20–10. Sensing an emotional surge among his players, Coach Fontes shouted that they were going for the win and ordered a squib kick, even though more than six minutes were left.

When the Lions kickoff team stacked most of the players to one side of the field in preparation for an onside kick, the stunned Vikings had no time to adjust. In a mad scramble, tight end Derek Tennell collapsed on the ball at the Lions 43 yardline. Deftly alternating a short passing game with Barry's runs, the Lions steadily moved down the field and scored on a 16-yard pass to Willie Green to draw within three points. Jubilant fans could sense the surge of adrenalin that swept through the Lions, long a doormat in the NFL.

When a charged-up Lions defense forced the Vikings to punt after three plays, Sanders and Peete returned for one final drive. Cheering spectators, ecstatic over the gutsy determination displayed by both their offense and defense, wildly shouted and waved as the Lions offense approached the line of scrimmage.

Mitch Albom watched in stunned fascination

from the press box as Sanders rose to the occasion. "Has there ever been a guy like this," wrote Albom, "who goes through defenses like a school kid racing through the forest, his shirttail flying, his legs churning, shirking tacklers as if they were heavy trees rooted to the earth?"

Sanders drove the Lions down to the 15 yardline. The Vikings defense suspected a pass on the next play, but Peete confounded them by calling a draw play to Sanders. The runner, in Albom's words, "beat all five Vikings trying to stop him on that last draw play, going 15 yards of highlight film and ducking under the intimidating Joey Browner to cross the stripe and hang six on the scoreboard."

Rather than absorb another loss, the Lions bounded off the field with a 24–20 victory. In those last seven minutes, Sanders rushed for 70 yards—including picking up 6 key first downs—added 15 yards in short passes, and scored the winning touchdown. Offensive tackle Lomas Brown, who struggled through years of misery, gushed that he had never before experienced a victory like this one and said of Sanders, "I *loooove* blocking for that guy."

Rodney Peete later compared the game to the one every player dreams about, where your team seems hopelessly defeated yet you bring them back to victory. "It's the kind of game you

After offensive lineman Mike Utley was paralyzed, the Lions banded together and dedicated one of their best seasons in his honor.

The Washington Redskins slammed Detroit's hopes of getting to the Super Bowl by crushing them in the 1992 NFC championship game. Here linebacker Wilber Marshall stops a determined Barry Sanders in first-quarter action.

always look forward to," Peete said. Now, though, "I'll be able to look back instead of forward."

When asked if Sanders, who normally maintained the same quiet composure through victory or defeat, appeared elated, Peete replied Sanders must have been excited. "I actually saw him smile in the huddle."

The fans who stuck it out to the end departed with a feeling that maybe, for a change, this Lions team held promise. Behind its explosive running back, rather than expecting a depressing season, the Lions could look ahead to challenging for the playoffs. As Albom wrote the next day, "This was the day the Lions truly grew up, shed their old skin."

With Sanders getting the ball more than 21 times a game, the supercharged team swept through the last six games undefeated and earned the team's first playoff appearance in twenty years. In those six games Sanders picked up 646 yards, including 220 and 4 touchdowns in a rematch against the Vikings.

One tragedy marred the playoff drive. On November 17 offensive lineman Mike Utley failed to get up from the ground after a scoring play. When officials and teammates ran to his side, they found Utley was paralyzed from the chest down as a result of an injury to his spine. As he left the field on a stretcher, the huge man gave a thumbs-up signal with his hand to teammates wishing him the best. For the rest of the season, the Lions adopted Utley's thumbs-up as a symbol of their commitment to a close friend and to excellence in play.

More so than many, Sanders was moved by the injury to Utley, one of his offensive linemen. Carrying the deep religious convictions gained from his mother, Sanders is very active in Champions for Christ, a religious organization of athletes. He conducts weekly Bible classes and holds chapel services the morning of each game. To him, "football is not the most important thing in my life. Religion, my family, being at peace with myself—and then maybe football." Thus when he watched a fellow player go down with an injury and not get back up, Sanders would want to help, not because Utley is a football star but because he is a human being.

"Everyone should be treated with dignity," Sanders asserts. "To me, it does not matter how much money a person earns, or the type of work he does. I judge someone on his or her merits, on his or her character. That's the important thing." As he told sportswriter Albom, "I just prefer to watch people first, to see if their walk is as big as their talk."

Unlike some football stars who drop to one knee and mutter a "private" prayer in front of 50,000 fans and a national television audience, you will never see Sanders publicly display his religion. When he scores, he politely hands the ball to the nearest official and trots off the field. Sanders does not criticize any other style and claims he "used to love Billy (White Shoes)

Johnson, and the Washington Smurfs," players known for their exuberant posttouchdown actions.

As Fontes says, "Barry doesn't wear his beliefs on his sleeve. . . . He's not for show; he's for real."

And so were the Lions, who challenged the powerful Dallas Cowboys in the 1991 NFC Central Division Championship Game. Dallas entered the game with a confidence that comes from winning 11 of its last 14 games, but from the opening kickoff the Lions maintained complete control. Relying on the superb passing of quarterback Erik Kramer and a remarkable 45-yard touchdown run, in which Sanders turned an apparent short gain into a long score by twisting and turning through the Dallas defense, the Lions tromped to a 38–6 win, their first playoff victory in 35 long years.

"Restore the Roar" fever swept the Detroit area as its football team moved to venerable RFK Stadium in Washington, D.C., to face the NFC's Eastern Division Champions, the Washington Redskins. Should they defeat Washington, the Lions would move on to their first Super Bowl appearance ever.

Sanders started in strong fashion against the vaunted Washington defense and picked up 46 yards in the first quarter alone. However, after making a few adjustments, Washington checked Sanders the rest of the game (he finished with 44 yards in 11 carries) and forced the Lions to rely on Kramer's passing. Since his touch was nowhere near the week before, Washington advanced to the Super Bowl with a 41–10 win.

Though they had failed to make the championship game, the Lions were pleased with their 12–4 regular-season record, a new high for the team. Fontes's design to get the ball into Barry's hands more often—Sanders carried the ball 87 more times than in 1990—worked beautifully. Sanders topped the NFL by scoring 17 touchdowns, led the NFC with 1,855 total yards and finished second in rushing to Dallas's Emmitt Smith with 1,548 yards—only 15 yards behind Smith's total. For his endeavors, the NFL Players Association named Sanders the league's Most Valuable Player, and *Football Digest* chose him as its 1991 Player of the Year.

The promise held out to Lions fans when Sanders left the Oklahoma State campus was that he would help take the team to the playoffs. That feat had been acomplished in three years. The All-Pro nose tackle at the time, Jerry Ball, said of Barry Sanders, "In work ethic, character, discipline, in every way, he sets a standard for each and every one on this team." Players and coaches alike looked expectantly to the 1992 season.

The Lions stumbled to a disappointing 5-11 record that year, however, as the team's old nemeses—erratic blocking and untimely penalties—hampered their ability to score. Sanders added to his luster by rushing for 1,352 yards and gaining a spot on the All-Pro team.

Sanders continued his blazing pace in 1993. After ten games, the team battled for a playoff spot with a 7-3 record and Sanders led the NFL with 1,052 yards. During the annual Thanksgiving Day game at the Silverdome, this time against the Bears, Sanders severely injured his left knee in the third quarter and had to be removed.

Sanders has an ice pack on his knee after being injured in a game against the Bears in 1993.

The Lions, disheartened about the removal of their main offensive threat, dropped a close 10–6 contest. One of their longtime rivals, the Minnesota Vikings, came to town the next week and thoroughly dominated the game, stifling the hampered Lions offense in a 13-0 win. However, with postseason play on the line, Barry's teammates pulled out victories in three of the final four games to earn a spot against Green Bay, the team defeated by the Lions in the regular-season finale, 30–20. Since Sanders was due to return from his injury, and since the game would be played at the Silverdome, prospects appeared hopeful.

Sanders ran like he had never missed a moment's action. In 27 attempts, the runner picked up a personal playoff-high 169 yards, but sadly watched victory slip out of the Lions' grasp in the game's final moments when Green Bay scored a come-from-behind touchdown to win, 28–24.

In his first five seasons, Sanders showed that he most effectively leads the Lions through example rather than words. He is not the rah-rah type who constantly exhorts his teammates, but instead lets his actions on and off the field do his talking. He works hard during games and practices, keeps himself in superb condition, and never points a finger of blame.

Even though he is a quiet leader, Sanders displays a sense of humor frequently enough to keep his coaches and treammates loose, particularly his head coach. During one practice, Sanders walked off the field to where Coach Fontes stood and mentioned he did not think he could return. When a suddenly concerned Fontes asked if he were injured, Sanders answered, "No. But the guys are using some awfully foul language out there. I don't know if I can stand it."

The astonished head coach stared in disbelief for a moment, unsure of what he should do. After a minute of awkward silence, Sanders burst out in laughter at the prank and returned to the field.

Fontes cannot feel safe from Barry's wit even in his own office. Prominently displayed on Fontes's desk is a Bible, which the coach rarely reads because he becomes so absorbed in his football work. One October, Sanders walked in, pointed at the Bible and calmly reprimanded his boss for not reading the good book. When Fontes asked how he knew, Sanders pointed to a bookmark protruding from the pages and said, "Because this hasn't moved since August."

"Now I have to move the thing around so he doesn't bust me again," smiled Fontes.

In his rookie season, Sanders loved teasing then defensive coordinator Woody Widenhofer, who had been the head coach at the University of Missouri during Barry's senior year in high school. Of course, Missouri never gave Sanders a look, and after compiling an 18-43-1 record, Widerhofer resigned the same year Sanders won the Heisman. Sanders could not let that pass by. From time to time he would look over at Widenhofer and remark, "Hey, Coach, maybe if you guys had taken me, you'd still be at Missouri."

Sanders enjoyed his finest year as a professional in 1994, when he challenged Eric Dickerson's 1984 rushing record of 2,105 yards.

After opening the season with 120 yards in a victory over Atlanta at the Silverdome, Sanders struggled to 16 yards in 12 carries in a losing effort against the Vikings. He rebounded in vintage Sanders fashion the following week by confounding the Dallas Cowboys defense with 194 yards in a career-high 40 carries, an effort that pushed him beyond the 7,000-yard mark for his career and earned Sanders the NFC Offensive Player of the Week Award.

Following this 20–17 victory over one of the league's premier teams, the Lions stumbled to three straight defeats, two against lesser powers. Sanders, however, put on a display of running talent that had fans at both the Silverdome and at Tampa Bay shaking their heads in disbelief. In a home loss to the New England Patriots, Sanders executed a spectacular run in which he turned around one defender three times.

At Tampa Bay the next week, Sanders ripped off the longest run of his career by darting for an 85-yard gain, even though one of his shoes was torn off when he smashed into the line. He quickly veered toward the right sideline and, without losing a step even though he awkwardly ran off balance because of his missing shoe, outraced his pursuers for most of the field, causing Tampa Bay running back Errict Rhett to exclaim, "Not only can I not do the things Barry does, I can't even describe them."

The Lions continued an erratic year by winning the next two games, then dropping two of the next three to fall to a mediocre 5-6 record that threatened to dash playoff aspirations. Like his mercurial team, Sanders either churned up yards in huge chunks or scratched out a few. Seven times in the first eleven games he raced for more than 100 yards, including 194 against Dallas, 166 versus Tampa Bay, 167 against Chicago, and a team-record 237 yards in a victory over Tampa Bay that earned Sanders his second NFC Offensive Player of the Week Award. In between, opposing defenses stifled Sanders to untypically low outputs, such as 16 yards against the Vikings, 47 versus Green Bay, and 42 against the Bears. After these eleven games, Barry's 1,361 yards kept him within range of Dickerson's mark, one of the premier records to own.

Concerned that they might miss the playoffs, the Lions went on a tear and swept four of their last five games to win a wild-card position. Solid efforts in three of the games—188, 127, and 110 yards—not only established a new Lions' rushing record but put Sanders within 169 yards of the NFL record. He fell way short, however, by grinding out 52 tough yards in a season-ending loss to the Miami Dolphins. The record would have been nice, but more importantly to Sanders, his team again headed into postseason play with a 9-7 record.

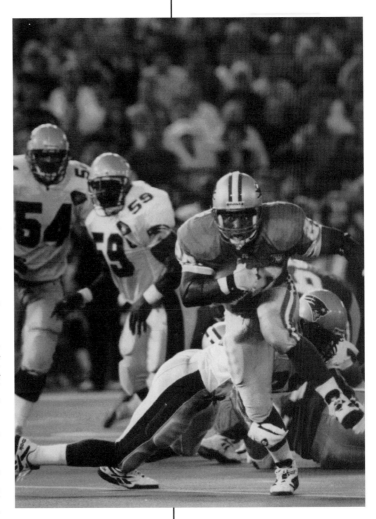

Myron Guyton of the New England Patriots has been unable to tackle Sanders, and Barry takes off on a 35-yard touchdown run.

With his low center of gravity, Sanders offers a small target for tacklers as Denetruys DuBose (number 93) of the Tampa Bay Bucs finds to his dismay.

Frustration once more haunted Detroit, who seemed unable to move beyond the early rounds. Visiting the cold of Green Bay on New Year's Eve, the Lions dropped a disappointing 16–12 game that featured the lowest single game output in Barry's career. Against a swarming Packer defense, Sanders rushed thirteen times for minus one yard.

For his exploits in 1994, Sanders was named the Associated Press Offensive Player of the Year. In spite of fierce competition from Steve Young, who set a new pass efficiency record; Jerry Rice, who set a career touchdown mark; and Cris Carter, who broke the record for most passes caught in a season, the *Football Digest* again selected Barry as its player of the year. Not only had he threatened Dickerson, but Sanders scampered to six runs of 60 yards or better while the rest of the league totaled only three.

Not surprisingly, Sanders credited his teammates for his personal gridiron success. "There are a lot of guys on this team that make me look good," he emphasized upon receiving *Football Digest*'s award. "I was able to reap the benefits of playing in a good offense with a good line, good receivers, and a good quarterback."

In 1995, Sanders and his teammates finished second in the Central Division, behind the Green Bay Packers, with a 10-6 record. They received a berth in the NFC Wild-Card playoffs but were routed by the Philadelphia Eagles.

Sanders and the Lions look ahead with high hopes to future years, and with good reason. Barry has rushed for more yards in his stellar seven-year NFL career (10,172 rushing yards for a 2,077 average each year) than any other back during that same span, a total that puts him sixth on the all-time list of running greats. He has been named to the Pro Bowl each year, and has helped lift the Lions to two NFC Central crowns and playoff spots in four of the last five years. As a result of this steady progress, Lions tickets are a tougher commodity in Detroit. During Barry's years Silverdome attendance has risen from 37,000 per game to 65,000, a hefty seventy-five percent increase.

One reason that Barry has shattered or tied 15 Lions offensive marks is his unheralded ability to hold onto the football. Barry coughed up the pigskin on December 6, 1992, against Green Bay and did not commit another turnover until the third game of the 1995 season. Until that time, he caught or carried the ball 803 times without a fumble.

Has all this fame changed Sanders? Not at all, according to his teammates, who tease him about his frugal ways. Close friend and teammate William White accompanied Sanders to an exclusive suburban men's store and almost fell over when Barry chose an English-style tweed jacket with patches. Telling Barry he needed something more fashionable, White watched as his wealthy teammate first settled on two suits, then switched to a blazer and two pairs of

Football Digest *named Barry Sanders as its Player of the Year in 1994, but once again Detroit was quickly bounced out of the playoffs, this time by the Green Bay Packers.*

slacks because it was less expensive. "Everything he looked at, he still checked the inside sleeve for the price," the amused White related to Mitch Albom. Lions defensive back, Bennie Blades, loves to claim that "if they still made the Pinto? Barry would be driving a Pinto, guaranteed."

Sanders smiles at the kidding, but agrees that he lives on about $30,000 of his huge salary and puts the remainder into his savings or shares it with family and charities. One thing that teammates agree on is that he does not put money into food. White relates that if you visited Barry's home and checked the refrigerator, "all he has in there is apple juice, water, and banana pudding. And maybe some four-month-old milk."

It is rare to find an athlete so supremely talented on the field, yet so unassuming off it. While the quiet Sanders may not bask in the limelight or allow strangers to get too close a glimpse into his personal side, we have the pleasure of watching Sanders weave his miracles with a football on crisp Sunday afternoons.

At least in that, we share a common trait with NFL players like running back Ricky Watters, formerly of the San Francisco 49ers but more recently of the Philadelphia Eagles. One of the league's most exciting runners himself, Watters unhesitatingly states Sanders operates upon a different plane than other backs. "When we play the Lions and their offense is on the field, I'm right there looking at what Barry's doing. He's the measuring stick."

CHRONOLOGY

1968   Born in Wichita, Kansas, on July 16.

1985   Plays tailback as a senior at Wichita North High School and gains 1,417 rushing yards in half a season. Named to the All-State team.

1988   Leading Oklahoma State University to a 10-2 record, Barry breaks or ties 24 NCAA records. Wins the Heisman Trophy.

1989   Selected in the first round of the NFL draft by the Detroit Lions. Gains 1,470 yards, second in the NFL by only 10 yards. Named NFL Rookie of the Year. Chosen to play in the Pro Bowl.

1990   Captures the NFL rushing title with 1,304 yards. Chosen to play in the Pro Bowl.

1991   Helps lead Lions to an NFC Central Division championship with a 12-4 record. Rushes for 1,548 yards and a league-leading 17 touchdowns. Receives *Football Digest*'s Player of the Year Award. Named the NFL Players Association NFC Most Valuable Player.

1992   Finishes second in the NFC with 1,352 yards rushing. Starts his fourth consecutive Pro Bowl. Sets the Lions' career rushing record.

1993   Misses final five regular-season games, but still rushes for more than 1,000 yards (1,115) for the fifth straight year. Gains 169 yards rushing in playoff game against the Green Bay Packers. Selected for the Pro Bowl.

1994   Rushes for 1,883 yards, the fourth-highest total in NFL history. Sets a Lions' single-game record with 237 rushing yards against Tampa Bay. Named Associated Press Offensive Player of the Year. Named *Football Digest*'s Player of the Year for the second time.

1995   Named to seventh straight Pro Bowl.

STATISTICS

BARRY SANDERS

COLLEGE

YEAR	RUSHING					RECEIVING			
	NO	YDS	AVG	TDS		NO	YDS	AVG	TDS
1986	74	325	4.4	2		0	0	0	0
1987	111	622	5.6	9		4	58	14.7	1
1988	344	2,628	7.6	37		19	106	5.6	0
TOTALS	529	3,575	6.8	48		23	164	7.1	1

PROFESSIONAL

YEAR	RUSHING					RECEIVING			
	NO	YDS	AVG	TDS		NO	YDS	AVG	TDS
1989	280	1,470	5.3	14		24	282	11.8	0
1990	255	**1,304**	5.1	13		35	462	13.3	3
1991	342	1,548	4.5	**16**		41	307	7.5	1
1992	312	1,352	4.3	9		29	225	7.8	1
1993	243	1,115	4.6	3		36	205	5.7	0
1994	331	**1,883**	5.7	7		44	283	6.4	1
1995	314	1,500	4.8	11		48	398	8.3	1
TOTALS	2,077	10,172	4.9	73		257	2,162	8.4	7

NO	number
YDS	yards
AVG	average
TDS	touchdowns

bold indicates league-leading figures

Suggestions for Further Reading

Gutman, Bill. *Barry Sanders: Football's Rushing Champ.* Brookfield, CT: The Millbrook Press, 1993.

Kavanagh, Jack. *Barry Sanders: Rocket Running Back.* Minneapolis: Lerner Publications, 1994.

LaBlanc, Michael L., ed. *Contemporary Black Biography.* Vol. I. Detroit: Gale Research, 1992.

Reiser, Howard. *Barry Sanders: Lion with a Quiet Roar.* Chicago: Children's Press, 1993.

About the Author

John F. Wukovits is a teacher and writer from Trenton, Michigan, who specializes in sports and World War II history. His work has appeared in over twenty-five different publications, including *PGA Magazine* and *Sports History.* His earlier books include a biography of World War II admiral Clifton Sprague and an account of the 1945 battle of Okinawa. A graduate of the University of Notre Dame, Wukovits is the father of three daughters—Amy, Julie, and Karen.

INDEX